The PAINTER & ROSE

Eva Howarth

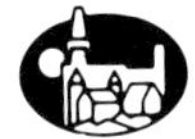

Salem House Publishers
Topsfield, Massachusetts

Created and produced by
PHOEBE PHILLIPS EDITIONS

First published in the United States
by Salem House Publishers, 1989,
462 Boston Street, Topsfield, Massachusetts 01983

ISBN 0 88162 458 6

Design: Caroline Reeves
Typeset by J&L Composition Ltd
Colour origination by Columbia Offset
Printed in Italy by Rotolito Lombarda

Introduction to

The PAINTER and The ROSE

The story of the Queen of Flowers told through seven centuries of art, their glorious colours and delicious full-blown beauty celebrated by 22 of our best-loved artists, from Nicholas Hilliard and Pieter Brueghel to Manet and Renoir.

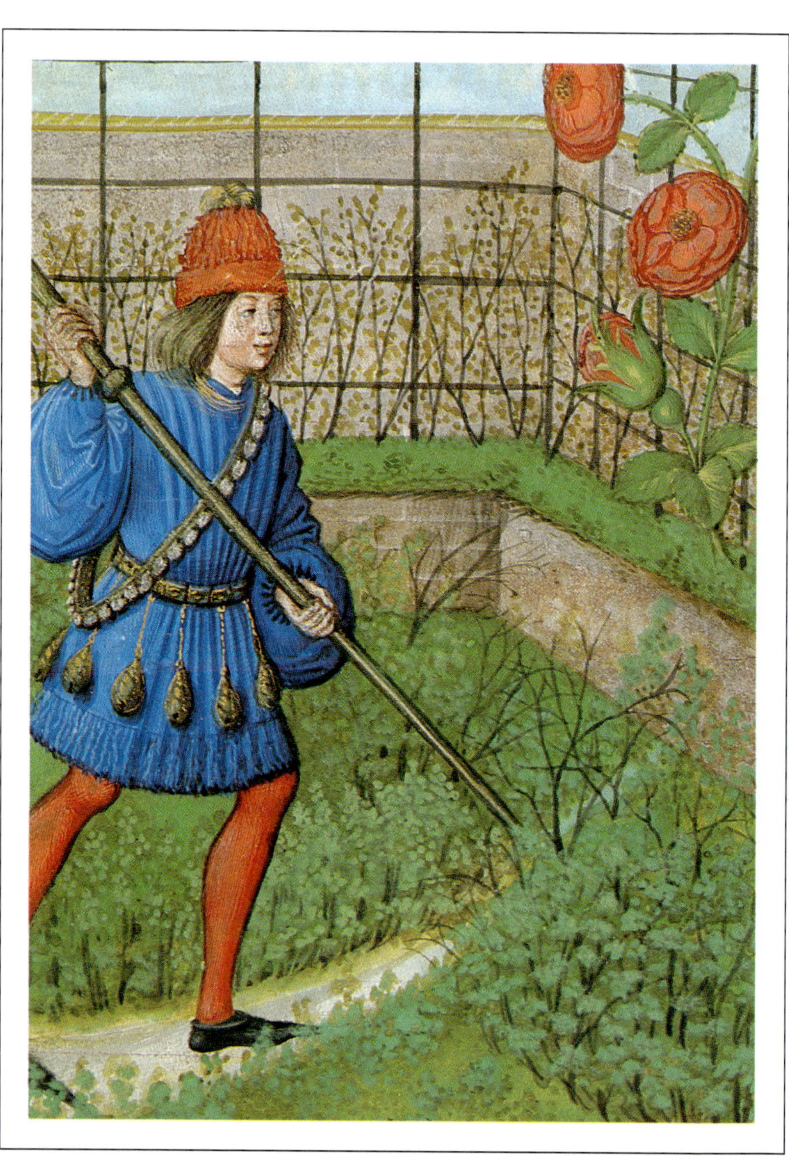

The Lover Attains the Rose

Flemish c. 1500 — Harley MS, British Library, London

The painting is an illustration from *Le Roman de la Rose*, a thirteenth-century French poem which ran to nearly 20,000 lines. The central figure is a lover, who is searching for the rose, the symbol of the perfect woman.

His search brings him to a park, where he meets with various difficulties and distractions. He finds Pleasure and Delight and Cupid, but Danger, Shame, Scandal and Jealousy all intervene in various ways.

The park in which the lover seeks the rose is divided, as was common in the Middle Ages, into a number of small gardens, separated by walls or hedges and linked by gates, bridges or steps.

In one garden there is grass; in another a fountain which feeds a stream. Each garden has a surprise, and is different from all the others. In the last garden the lover finds the rose and meets Welcome, who gives him permission to kiss it.

The poem demonstrates the place of honour accorded to the rose in medieval times, not only as the symbol of love, but also as the queen of garden flowers.

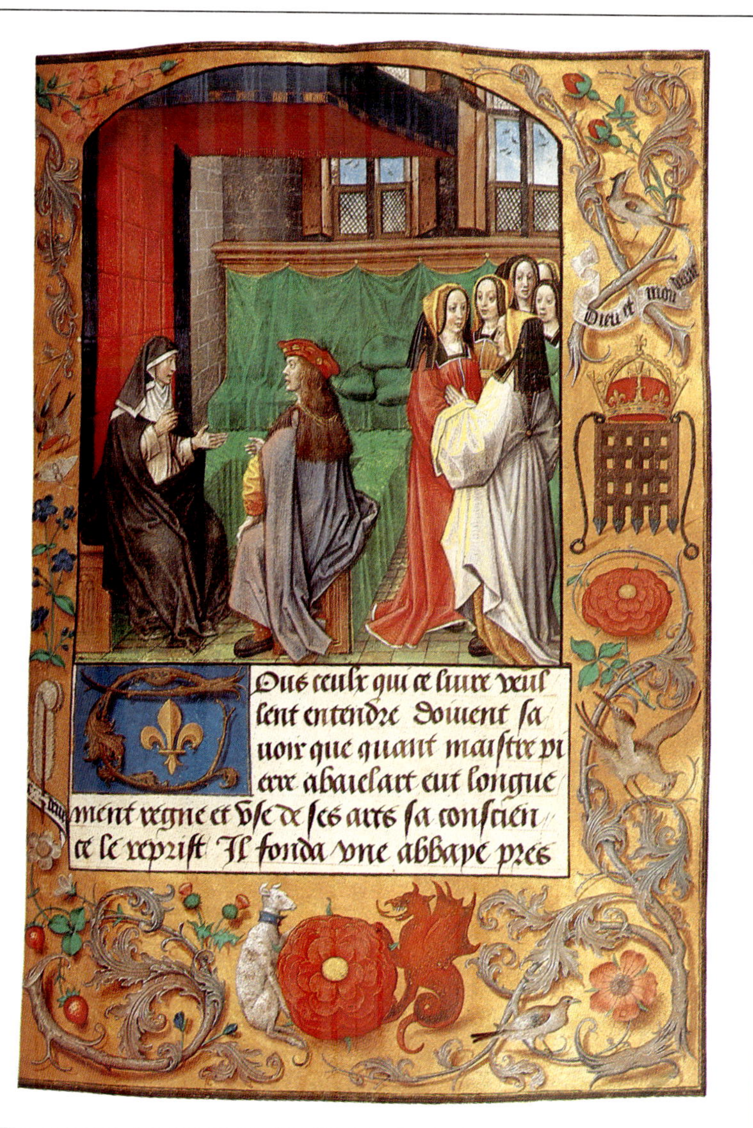
Dieu et mon droit
Ous ceulx qui ce liure veul
lent entendre doiuent sa
uoir que quant maistre pi
erre abaielart eut longue
ment regne et vse de ses arts sa consien
ce le reprist Il fonda vne abbaye pres

Abelard and Héloïse

French | Royal MS, British Library, London

The monk in the painting is Peter Abelard, who lived in the twelfth century and was regarded in France as the most learned man of his time. The nun is Héloïse, whom he secretly married. Their tragic affair was one of the great love stories of the Middle Ages.

The Church at that time had a virtual monopoly of learning, and medicine, for instance, was largely dispensed by monks, who had their own herb gardens. Roses were commonly used for medicinal purposes, as they have been through the centuries in most civilizations.

Rose petals were thought to have cured Cyrus, King of the Medes and Persians, while the Greeks used them as a remedy against the bite of a mad dog. The Romans thought a rose petal floating in wine reduced the likelihood of a hangover and considered rose hips curative for gall bladder and kidney complaints. These were extreme cases, but there continues to be evidence that roses, and rose hips in particular, have valuable medicinal properties.

Rose hips are a rich source of Vitamin C and during World War II some 500 tons of rose hips as well as large quantities of dried rose petals were collected in Britain for the manufacture of drugs.

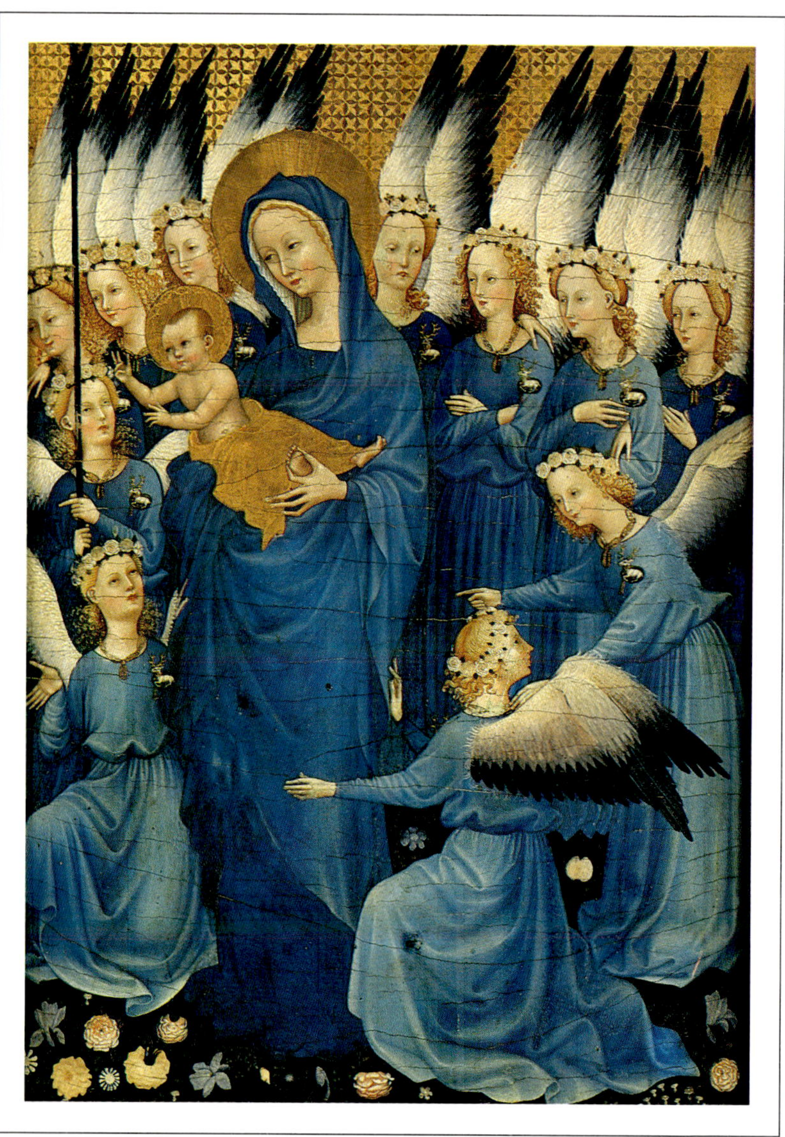

The Wilton Diptych

*c.*1400 National Gallery, London

In medieval paintings roses were commonly used to symbolize purity and thus, in the Wilton diptych, the angels have roses in garlands over their loosely flowing hair. In a number of other paintings the Madonna is shown in a field of small, multi-coloured roses.

This is, of course, in contrast to the earlier symbolism of Greece and Rome, in which the rose was directly associated with Venus Aphrodite, the goddess of love – a love which was indisputably and unashamedly erotic.

The symbolism was to be reversed once again in more modern times – for instance, Swinburne wrote of 'the lilies and languors of virtue, the roses and raptures of vice'.

Another common feature of medieval religious paintings seen in the Wilton diptych is the relative use of blue and gold. These were the most expensive pigments, blue being produced from lapis lazuli. The deepest blue, requiring the most pigment, was normally reserved for the Madonna herself, other less important figures being thought to merit smaller quantities.

When a painter was commissioned his contract often specified the amount of gold and blue he was to use. The quantity decided on reflected the status of the patron.

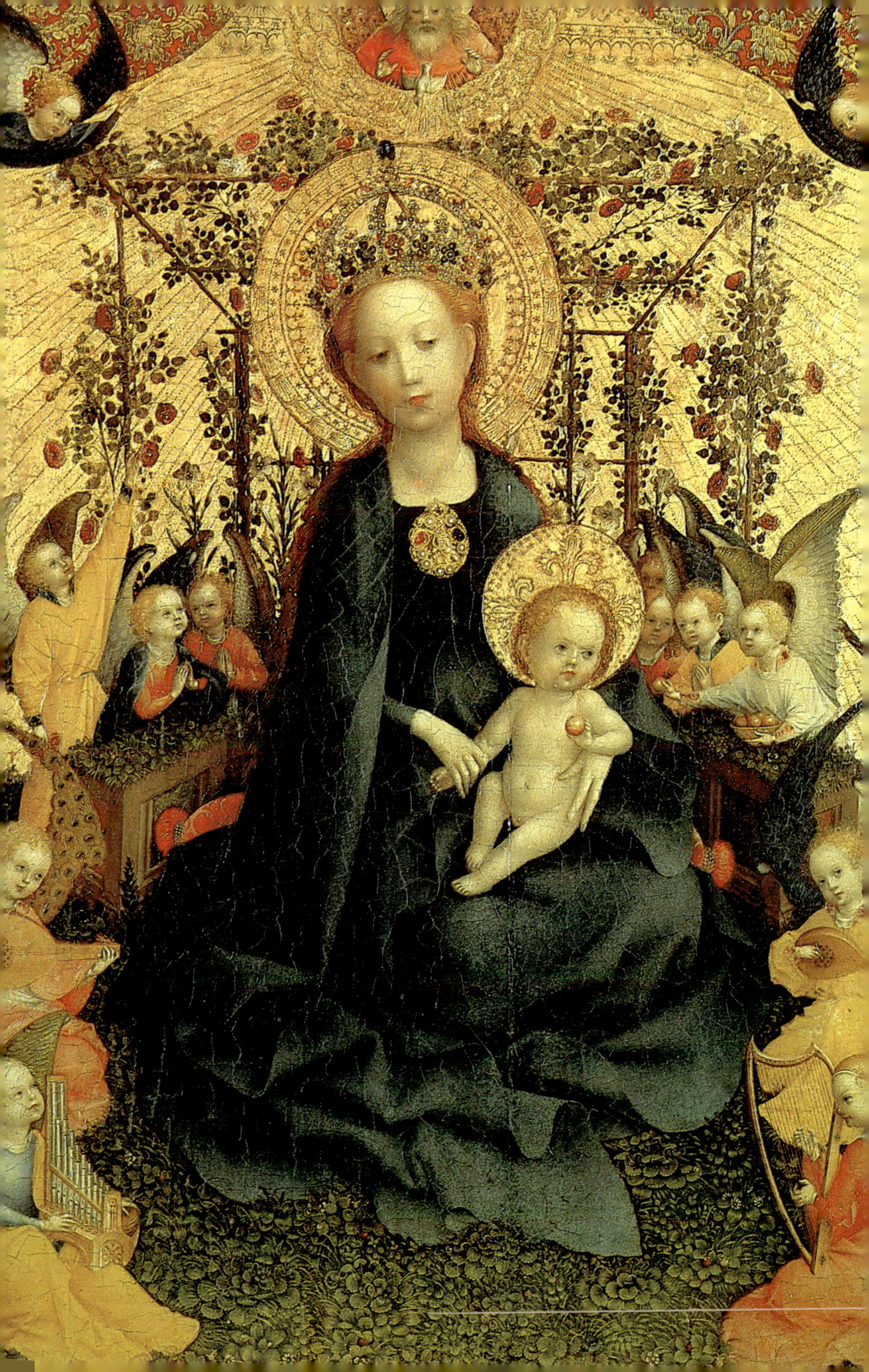

The Virgin in the Rose-Bower

Stefan Lochner

German c. 1410–1451 Wallraf-Richartz Museum, Cologne

Lochner spent most of his working life in Cologne. He is best known for his altar-pieces, in which the Madonnas he painted were fair and gentle. As in this picture, they were often portrayed in rose gardens with saints and angels playing musical instruments.

It was a papal custom in medieval times to give presents of red-tinted golden roses; the red was held to symbolize Christ's passion and the gold his kingship. Later it became the practice for popes to present jewelled roses, which were blessed on Rose Sunday.

The first recorded papal presentation of such a rose was to a Count of Anjou in 1096. The gift was intended to encourage the Count to take part in the First Crusade. Individual gifts of the golden rose were also made to women, including Isabella of Spain, Catherine de Medici, Mary Tudor and the Empress Eugénie of France.

Among the more recent recipients was the Grand Duchess of Luxembourg, who received a golden rose in 1956.

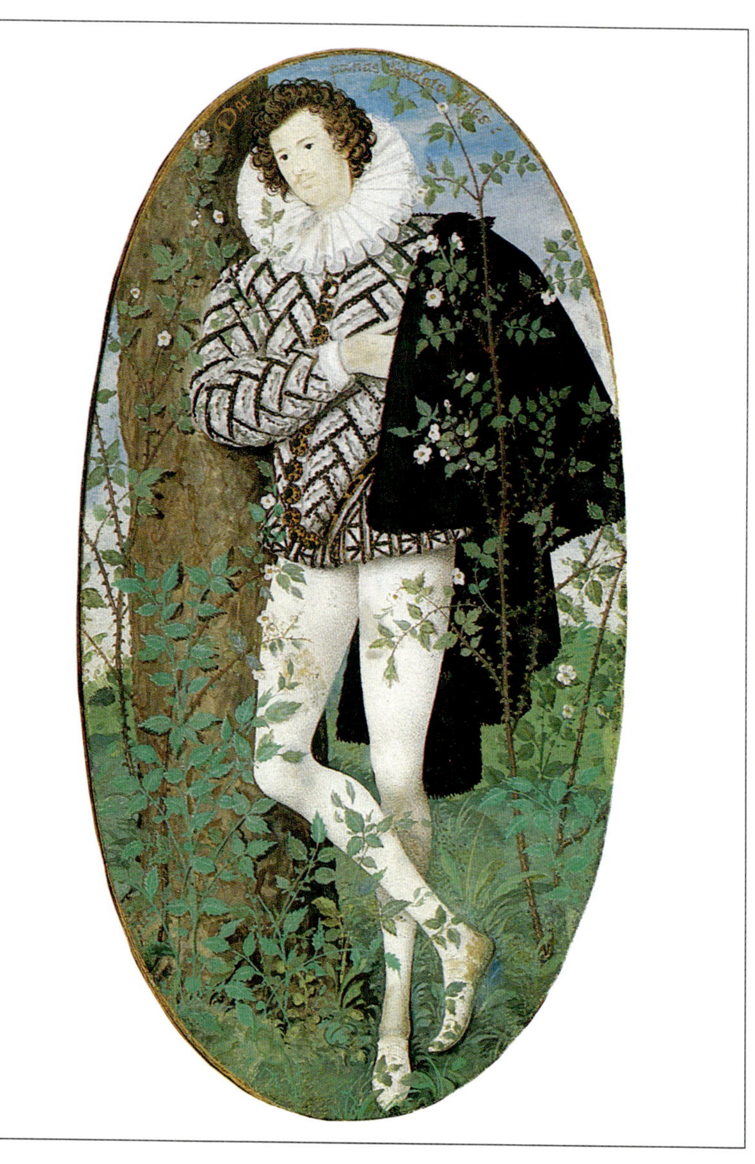

Young Man Among the Roses

Nicholas Hilliard

English 1547–1619 Victoria and Albert Museum, London

The portrait of the unknown young man was painted in miniature, a form of art which became popular at the court of Queen Elizabeth I. Miniatures in elaborate frames were given as presents or love tokens and were worn as jewels.

Hilliard, a contemporary of Shakespeare, was perhaps the most important native-born English artist of the sixteenth century.

In this miniature the thorns of the rosebush play as important a part as the roses themselves. The roses of course symbolize love, and the thorns pain or death.

The message is clear – the young man is expressing his love and at the same time the pain he will feel if he is rejected, a feeling echoed in many of Shakespeare's sonnets.

The expression 'a rose without a thorn' has long been used to mean perfection. In the fourth century a bishop named Basil announced that in the Garden of Eden the roses had no thorns until Adam and Eve were expelled.

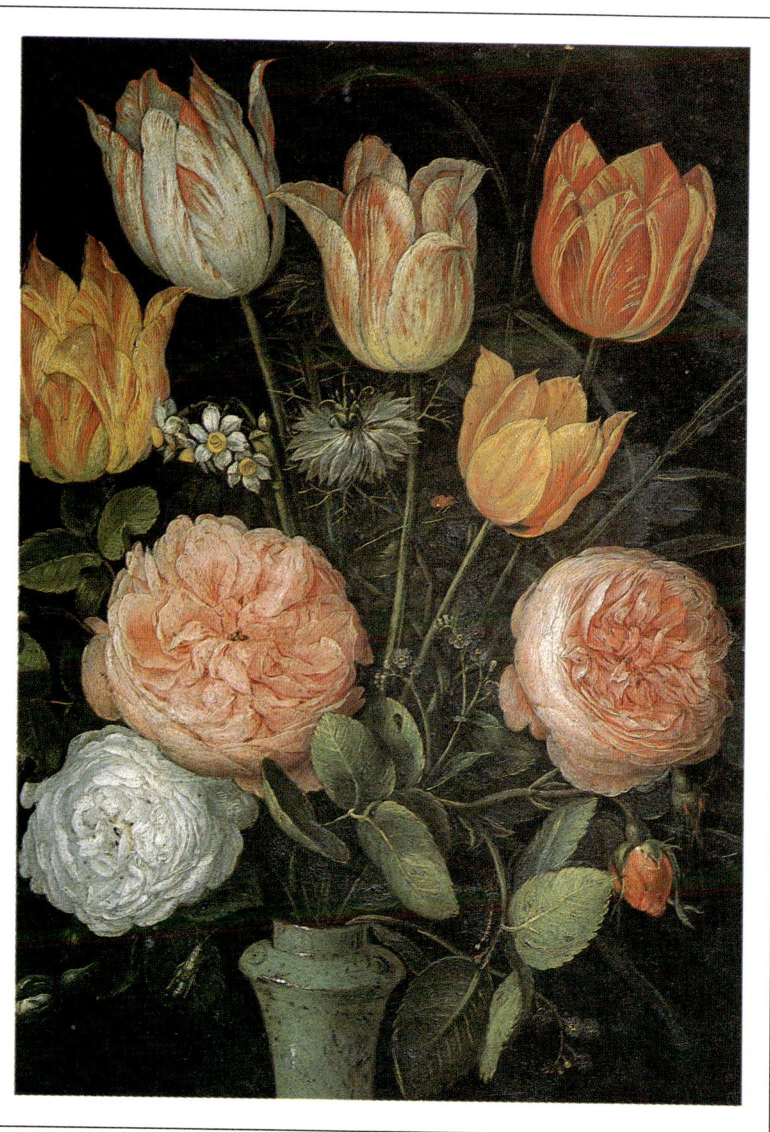

Roses with Diamonds

Jan Brueghel

Flemish 1568–1625 Galleria dell'Accademia Carrara, Bergamo

Jan Brueghel came from a famous family of Flemish painters, of whom his father, Pieter, was the most celebrated.

As a painter of flowers Jan Brueghel was unsurpassed in his time. He even became known as Velvet Brueghel because of the extraordinary skill with which he conveyed the texture both of silks and of flowers.

Most of the great flower paintings of the sixteenth and seventeenth centuries were Dutch or Flemish, and it is curious that the cabbage or hundred-leaf rose (*Rosa centifolia*) does not appear in any of them.

This has led historians to conclude that when Jan Brueghel was painting the cabbage rose had not yet made its appearance in the Low Countries or, if it had, that it was still a rarity. It began to appear in paintings by Jan Brueghel's successors in the seventeenth century.

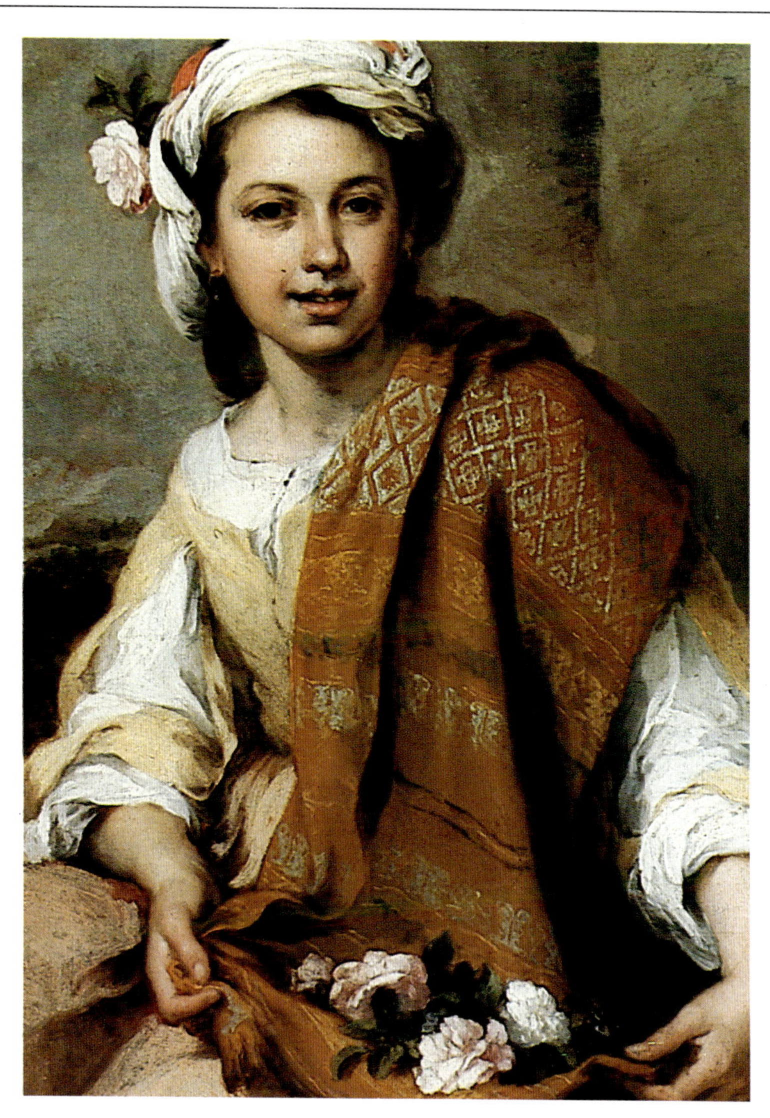

The Flower Girl

Bartolomeo Esteban Murillo

Spanish 1617–1682 Dulwich Gallery, London

Children have always loved dressing up, and of all the classical Masters, Murillo was the most famous in later life for his idealized portraits of poor waifs. Often they were costumed in classical robes as models for religious paintings, any dirt easily hidden by bright linen and embroidery, but he was even more popular for his street scenes – two boys on the curbstones, eating a bunch of grapes, for example, or in this delightful portrait, fresh roses make the perfect excuse to call his model a flower girl. It is unlikely that the genuine street-seller was so well-fed or so obviously contented with life!

Idealized or not, one point is true to life – the Spanish appetite for roses and all rose products was and is enormous, especially around Seville where Murillo worked. The modern equivalant of his rose girl might carry rose water and candied rose petals for cooking, dried rosebud for pot pourri, and carefully wrapped long-stemmed roses for gentlemen to give their ladies in cafés and restaurants.

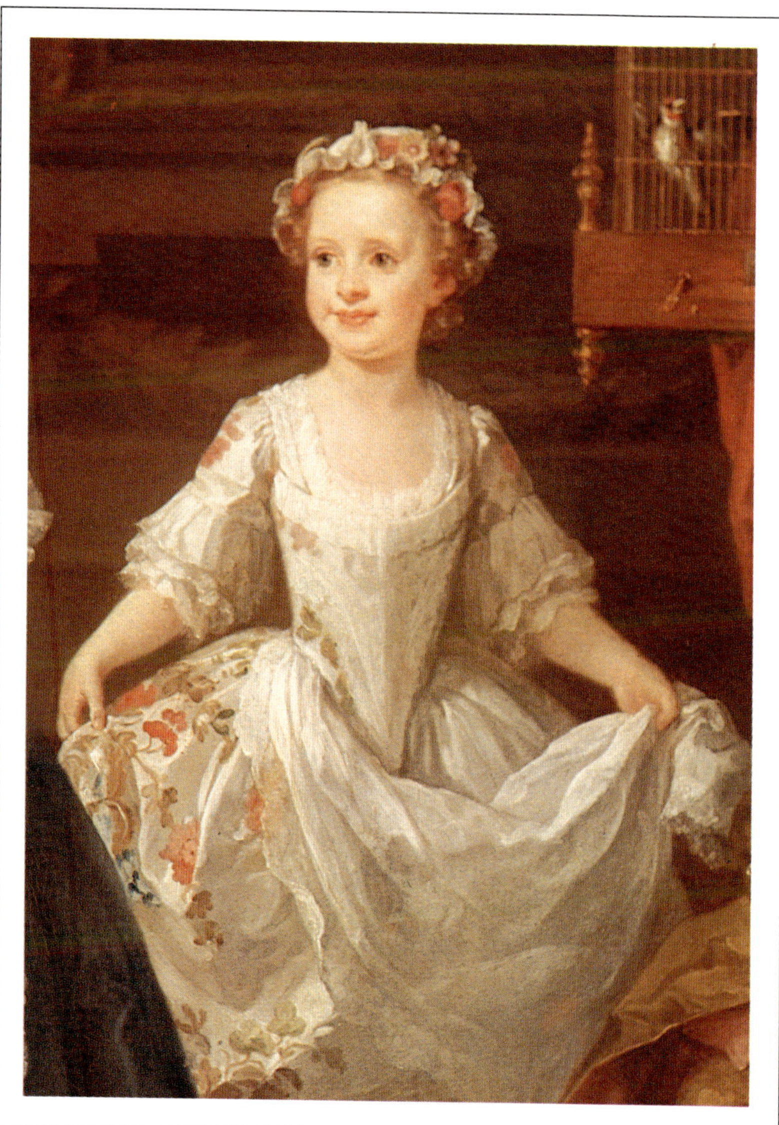

The Graham Children

William Hogarth

English 1697–1764 National Gallery, London

The girl in the painting is a daughter of Daniel Graham, apothecary at the Chelsea Hospital and a friend of Hogarth. She may well be dreaming of a man she will one day meet and marry.

Roses have often been used for love divinations. In parts of south-west England girls used to walk backwards into gardens on Midsummer Eve and pluck a rose.

The rose would then be sewn up in a paper bag and put in a dark drawer. On Christmas morning the girl would take the bag out, place the rose on her bosom and wear it to church. If a young man asked her for the rose – or took it without asking – she would know he was her future husband.

Roses have been used for foretelling the future in many other ways. One of the commonest European beliefs is that a profusion of roses heralds a severe winter.

In its light and bright colouring and its spontaneity the picture suggests the French rococo style, but Hogarth, who did not much care for foreign parts and resented foreign dominance in painting, might not have welcomed this suggestion.

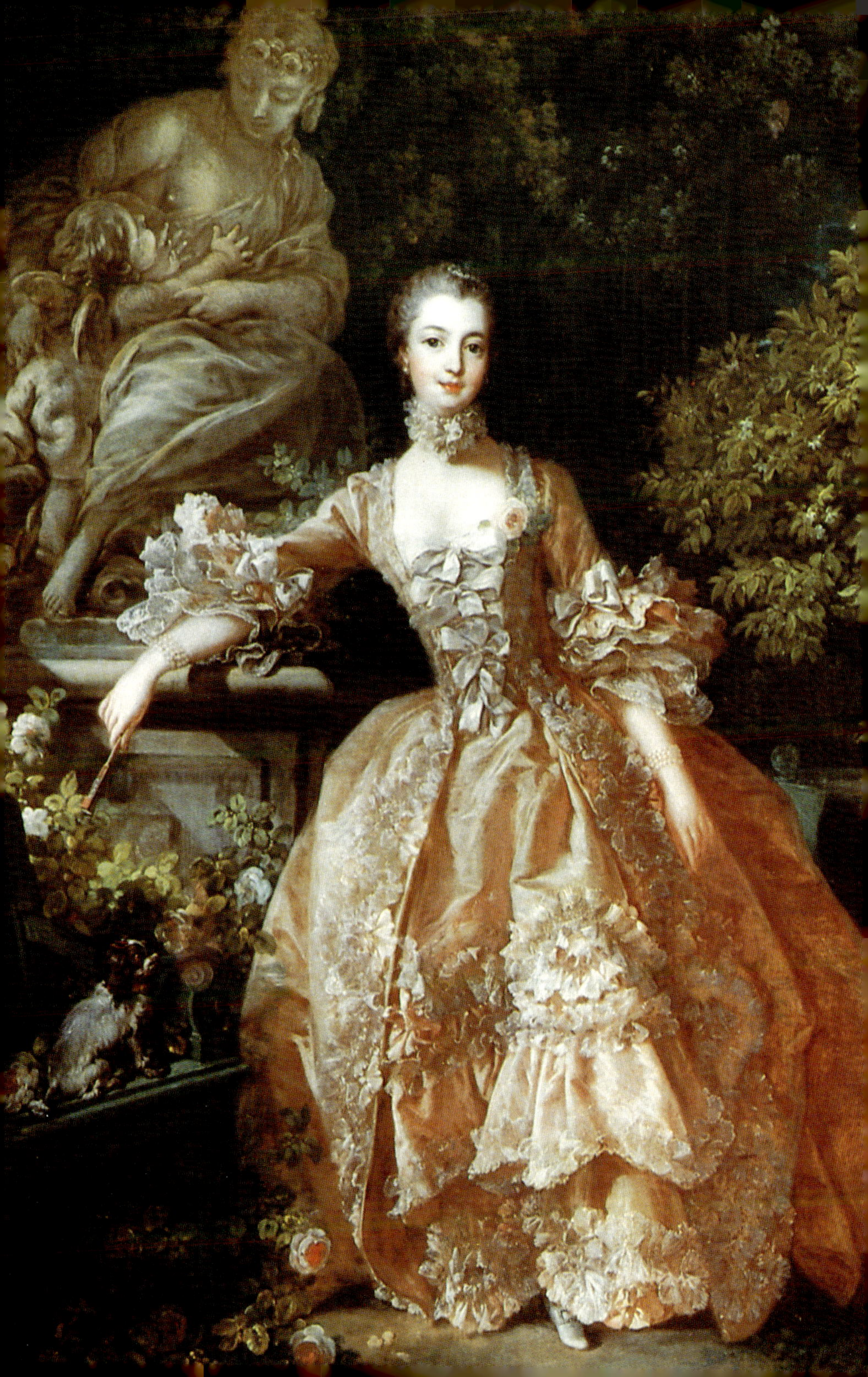

The Marquise de Pompadour

François Boucher

French 1703–1770 Wallace Collection, London

At the court of Versailles in the eighteenth century the rose was still the symbol of love. But it was no longer an innocent love, as Boucher's portrait of Madame de Pompadour makes clear.

Madame de Pompadour had been brought up from childhood to fill the coveted and exacting role of the King's mistress. When she achieved her ambition she rewarded a fortune-teller who had foretold her success with a pension for life. Unfortunately for her fellow-countrymen she very soon began to interfere in politics, acquired great power and used it to disastrous effect.

In Boucher's portrait Madame de Pompadour is presented as the Queen of Love. Roses surround her; they are at her feet, on her sleeves and on her décolletage. Even the flounces of her dress fall into the patterns of roses.

Boucher was a highly successful artist. He was officially styled the King's Painter and was a director of the Gobelin factory. Although he designed stage settings for operas and major decorative schemes for Versailles and Fontainebleau, it was as a portrait painter that he gained his great renown.

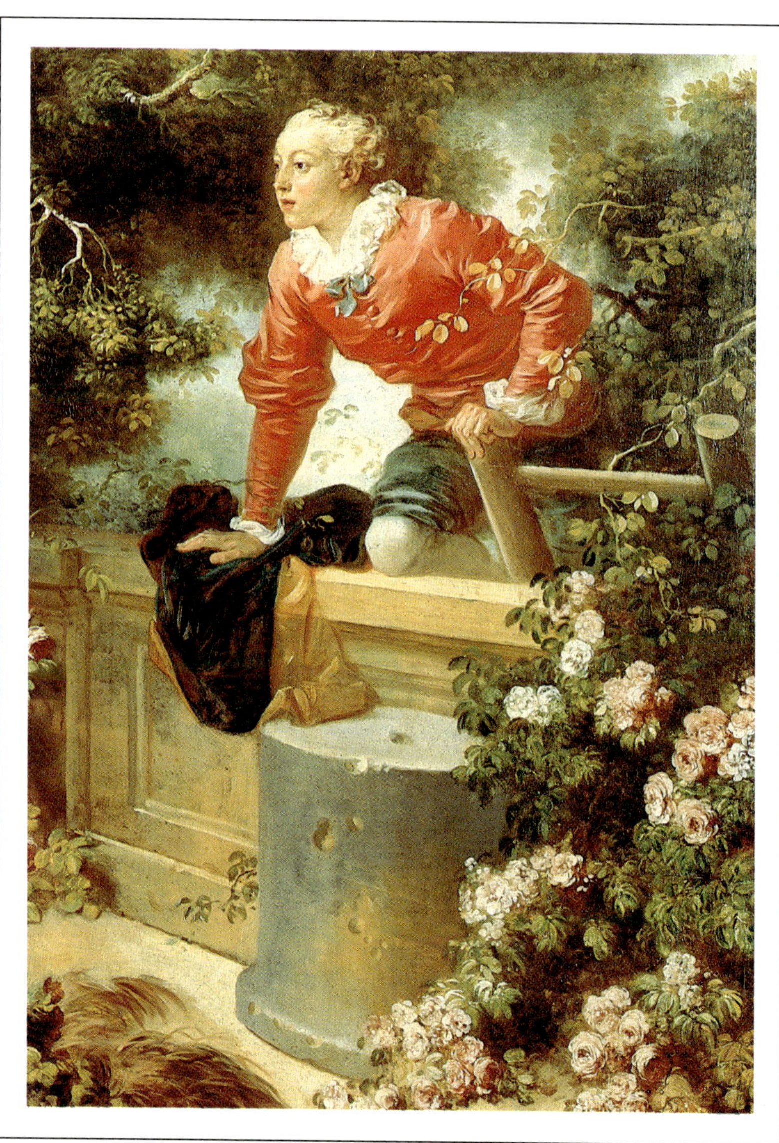

Storming the Citadel

Jean-Honoré Fragonard

French 1732–1806 Frick Collection, New York

Fragonard is best known as a painter of the erotic. Among his patrons were the royal mistresses, Madame de Pompadour and Madame du Barry.

He was born in Grasse, where the perfume industry has flourished since the sixteenth century; indeed, at one time Grasse provided the scent essence for half of Europe. The flowers, roses prominent among them, are grown in fields and greenhouses in the hills around Grasse. The roses must be freshly picked, and every morning large containers of their petals arrive at the scent factory.

Roses are an essential element of many famous perfumes such as Chanel No. 5, Crêpe de Chine, Shalimar, Arpège, Joy and Fête.

Avicenna, the great tenth-century Arab scientist, is believed to have been the first to extract the scent of roses by distillation. In the course of his experiments he produced the liquid known as rose-water.

In a number of countries in the Near and Middle East distinguished strangers are made welcome when they enter a home by having rose-water sprinkled over them.

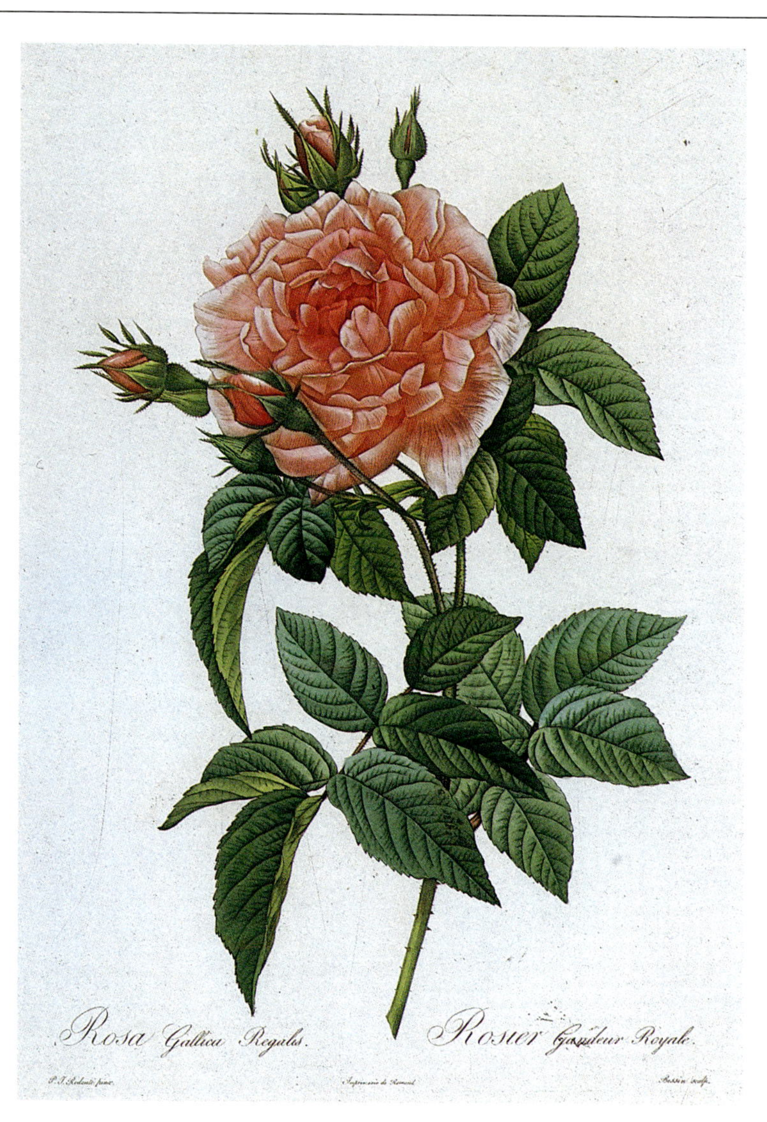
Rosa Gallica Regalis.
Rosier Gandeur Royale.
P. J. Redouté pinx.
Imprimerie de Rémond
Bessin sculp.

Rosa Gallica Regalis

Pierre-Joseph Redouté

French 1759–1840 The Royal Horticultural Society, London

Redouté is acknowledged as one of the greatest botanical painters of all time. He was also fortunate in that he was able to find favour in the highest circles throughout a turbulent period in French history. Queen Marie-Antoinette was his first important patron. After the Revolution he worked for Napoleon's first wife, Josephine, who created a glorious rose garden at Malmaison outside Paris. Napoleon's second wife, Marie-Louise, also patronized him. So, too, did Louis XVIII after the Bourbon restoration, and a number of the ladies at court became his pupils.

As this picture shows, Redouté was a meticulous painter with a deep knowledge of flowers. Roses naturally attracted him, not least because of their variety.

Redouté produced his most celebrated work, *Les Roses*, between 1817 and 1824. The first edition, which was printed on vellum, was limited to 500 copies. It included exquisitely painted water-colours of some 170 species and varieties of roses from Malmaison.

The book was dedicated to Redouté's most recent patroness, the Duchess de Barry.

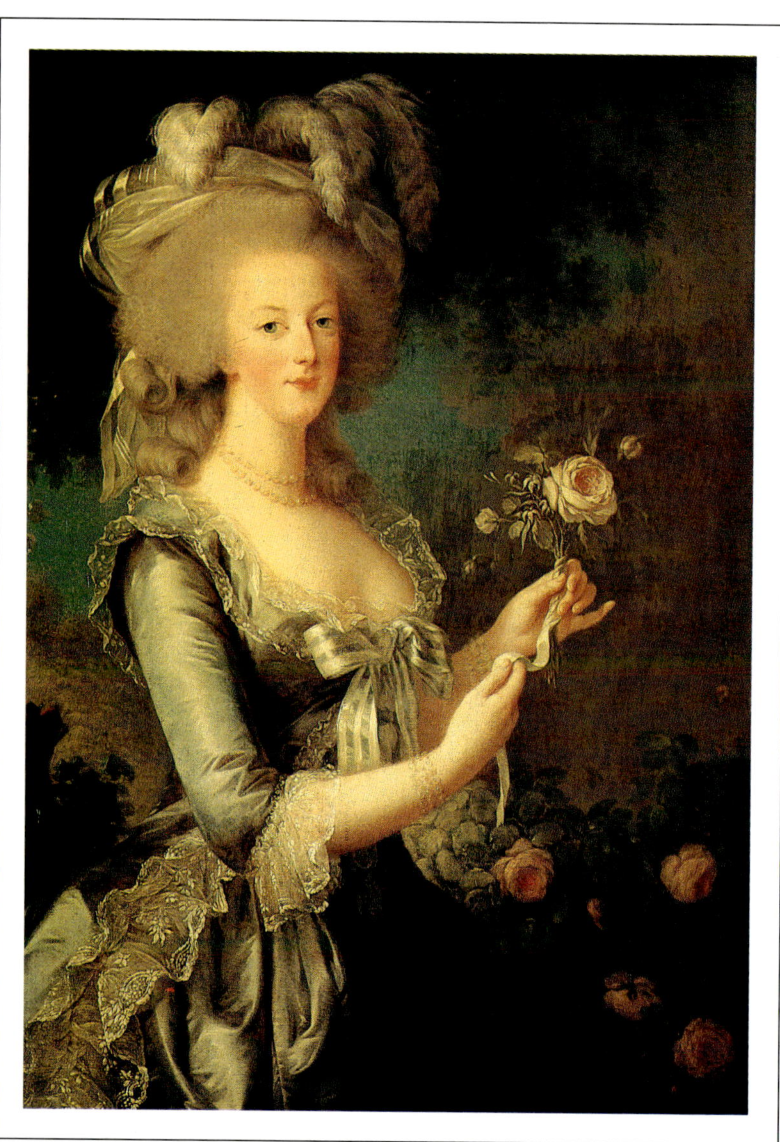

Marie-Antoinette

Élisabeth Vigée-Lebrun

French 1755–1842 Historical Museum, Versailles

The painter was on friendly terms with Louis XVI's Queen, Marie-Antoinette, and is believed to have painted her twenty-five times.

In the picture she is presented, not as a queen, but as a country lady admiring her roses. No doubt this pleased Marie-Antoinette, who delighted in what she imagined was rustic simplicity and even liked to think of herself from time to time as a simple shepherdess.

Roses have long been presented in France as prizes for beauty, virtue and artistic skill. At a festival founded in the sixth century in a village named Salency a crown of roses was awarded annually to the girl deemed to be the most beautiful, virtuous and pleasing.

Similar festivals were staged later in other parts of France. One of Maupassant's stories tells of a village where no girl whose virtue was beyond doubt could be found – so the prize was awarded to a young man, whose virginity was notorious and who was known to blush at the sight of a skirt!

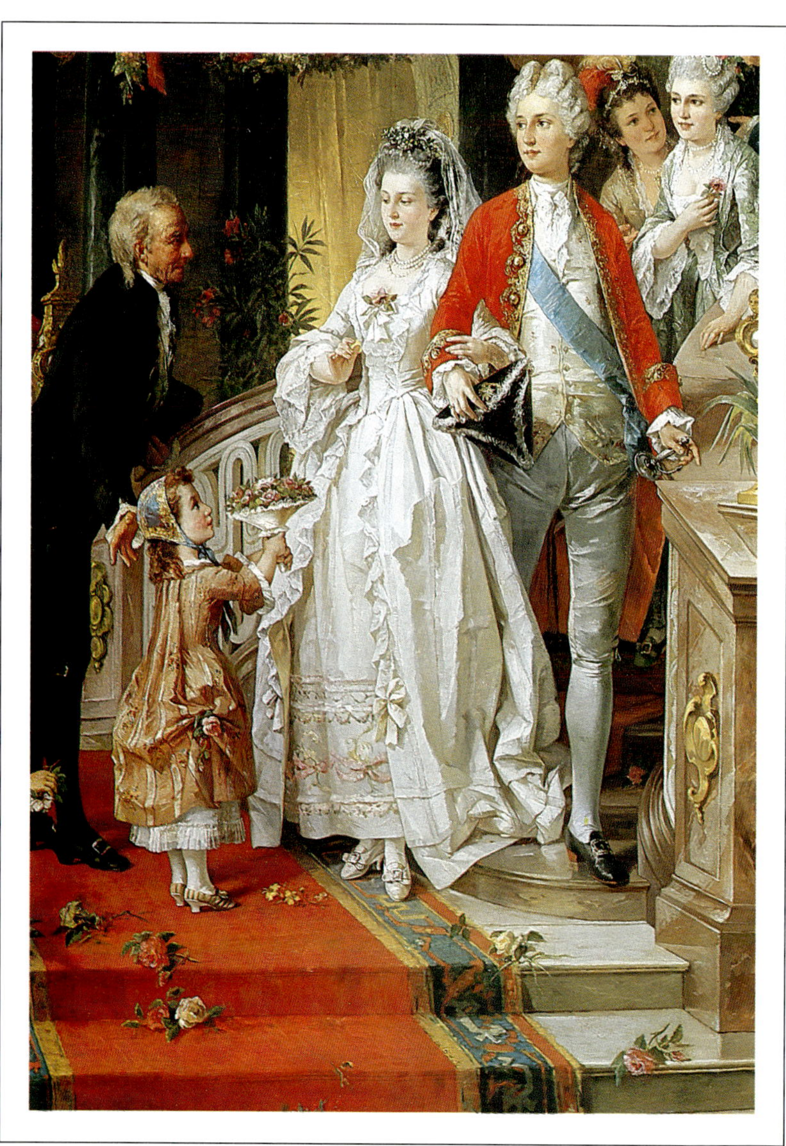

The Wedding Party

Carl Herpfer

French 1836–1897 — Private Collection

The home of the bride has been lavishly decorated with rose garlands. It is very likely, too, that one of the speech-makers will have expressed the hope that life for the bridal couple will be a bed of roses.

This expression could at one time be taken literally. The Sybarites, a people whose name has come to be associated with luxury and pleasure, did sleep on mattresses which were stuffed with rose-leaves.

Dionysius, the tyrant of Syracuse, also had his couch stuffed with roses, and the practice was not uncommon among the Romans, who also considered that a mattress stuffed with rose-leaves lessened the rigours of the journey when travelling on a litter.

The Emperor Nero in the first century AD chose rose petals as the ideal carpet for his banquets. He even had the sea shore of Naples covered with rose petals in preparation for his visit there.

Although the term 'bed of roses' has come to suggest improbable luxury, it is really no less logical to stuff a bed with rose-leaves than with birds' feathers.

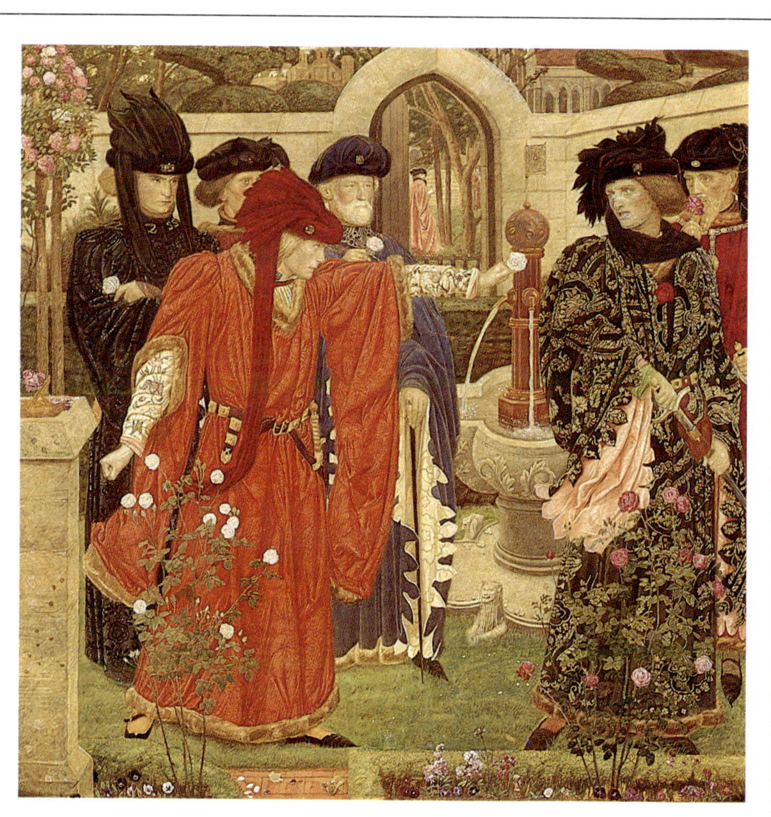

Choosing the Red and White Rose in the Temple Garden

Henry Payne

English 1868–1940 Birmingham City Museum, Birmingham

The rose is the national symbol of England. It was adopted as such in the fifteenth century, only after a prolonged civil war.

In Shakespeare's *Henry VI* (Part Two, Act Two, Scene Three) the setting is the Temple Garden, in London. Various noblemen enter, including the Earls of Somerset and Warwick.

Each of these noblemen belongs to one of two factions, whose leaders are contending for the throne of England. One faction is called the House of Lancaster, the other the House of York.

Somerset picks a red rose in the garden. This is the symbol of the Lancastrians. Warwick then picks a white rose, the Yorkist symbol.

This picking of roses is tantamount to a declaration of civil war, and Warwick says:

> I prophesy this brawl today,
> Grown to this faction in the Temple Garden,
> Shall send, between the red rose and the white,
> A thousand souls to death and deadly night.

Many more than a thousand were lost in a long and costly war. It was not really won by either side, but the eventual outcome of the factional differences was the establishment of the Tudor dynasty on the English throne.

There is still in existence today a red rose from Tudor times. It was found in Canterbury pressed between the leaves of a bible.

Henry Payne, the painter of the picture shown, was a follower of the Pre-Raphaelites.

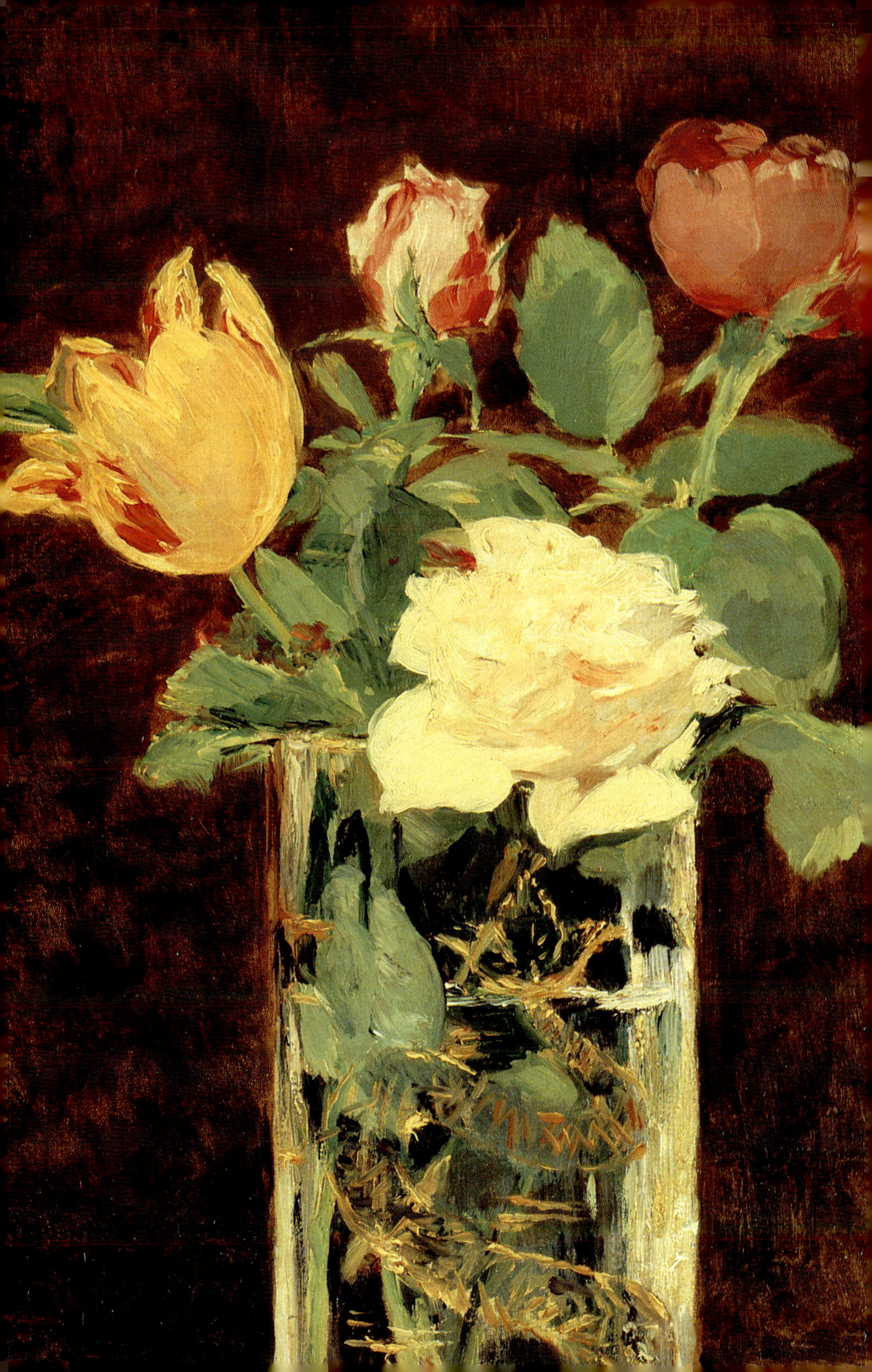

Roses and Tulips
Édouard Manet
French 1832–1883 Bührle Foundation, Zurich

According to a Romanian legend, the rose was a young and lovely princess who dazzled the sun with her beauty when she was bathing in the sea.

The sun covered her body with kisses and stayed gazing at her, and for three days running he forgot to vanish in the evening. As a result there was no night.

To make sure this did not happen again the ruler of the universe changed the princess into a rose. This explains why the rose hangs her head and blushes whenever the sun looks down on her.

Tulips, the other flowers in Manet's painting, have not given rise to legends in the same way as roses. But in the seventeenth century in the Netherlands there was an extraordinary outburst of speculation known as 'tulipomania'. Single roots fetched fantastic prices, and when the bubble burst a number of the speculators became bankrupt.

Manet, one of the greatest of the French impressionist painters, was a lover of roses. He was probably the only artist to make a practice of standing them in a glass of champagne when painting them!

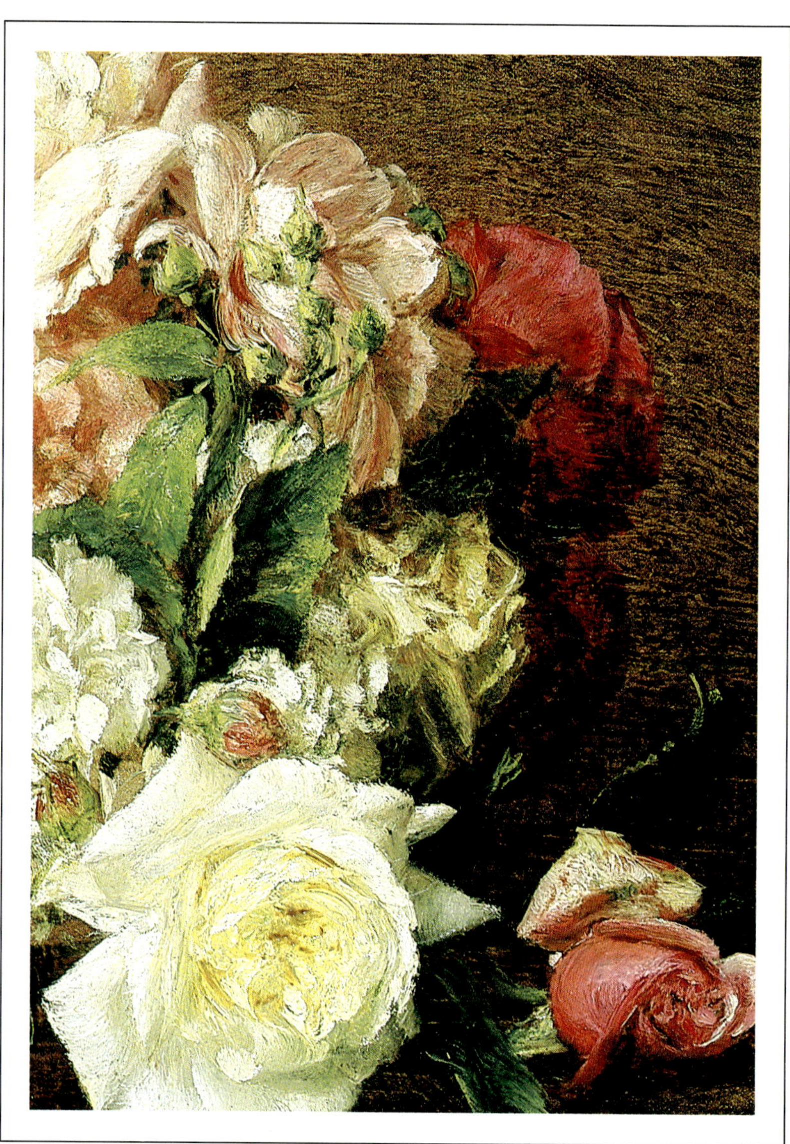

Roses

Henri Fantin-Latour

French 1836–1904 Private Collection

Fantin-Latour was most admired for his still-life paintings, particularly those of flowers. This picture is one of his most successful paintings of roses. The flowers are a riot of colour and vary in shade from the purest white to the deepest red. They are at the height of their beauty, in full bloom.

Fantin-Latour had numerous artist friends, among them Whistler, who introduced him to artistic circles in London. Later he became a frequent visitor to England, where his flower paintings were particularly admired.

Whistler features in one of his best-known paintings, *Homage to Delacroix*, a painter he greatly admired. Monet, Manet and Renoir, as well as Zola and Baudelaire, appear in others of his works.

He was also an admirer of Wagner, and made a number of drawings illustrating the works of leading nineteenth-century composers, Wagner, Brahms and Berlioz among them.

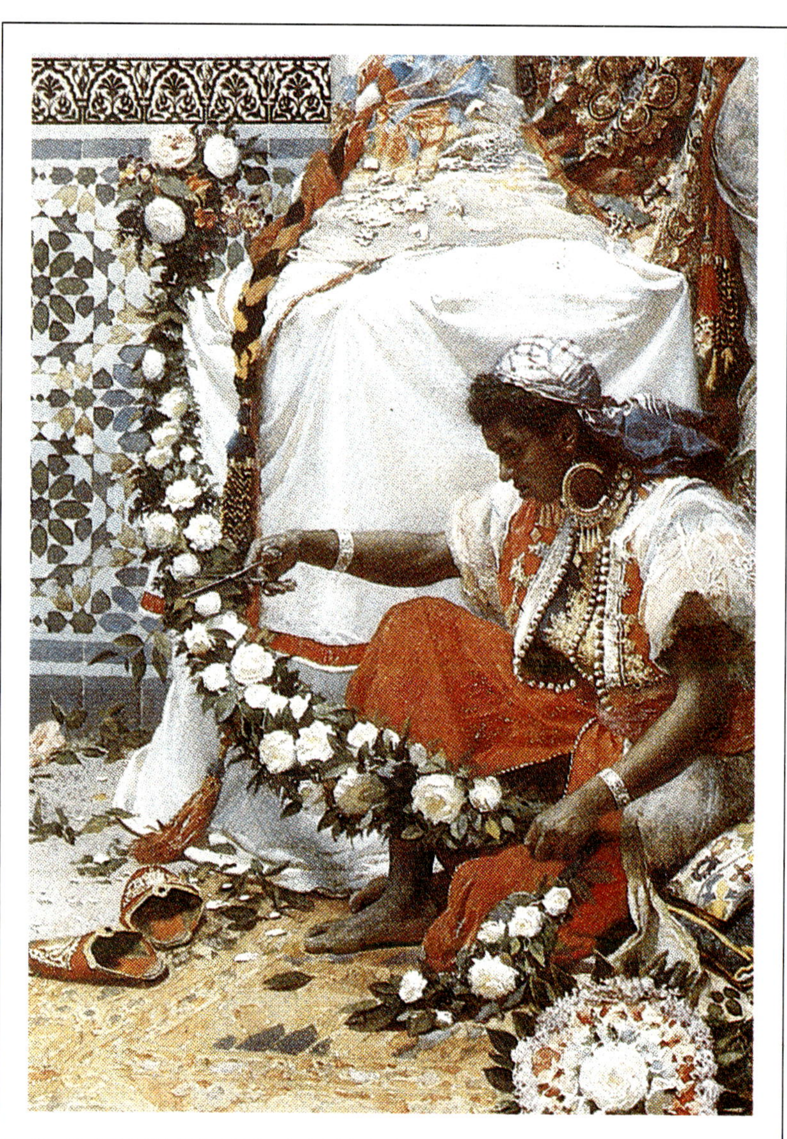

Wedding of the Sheikh of Tangiers's Daughter

Jose Tapiro y Baro

Spanish 1830–1913 Private Collection

In the nineteenth century a number of European painters, including Baro, were attracted by subjects which suggested the mysteries of the East.

In the painting an attendant is preparing a garland of roses for a bride.

The rose has long played an important part in Islamic culture. In Persian legend and poetry in particular it appears again and again, often in conjunction with the nightingale.

According to the Persian poet Attar, all the birds came to Solomon and complained that the nightingale had been disturbing their rest.

Solomon summoned the nightingale and asked him for an explanation. The nightingale said that he was so much in love with the rose that he had to express his feelings in song. Solomon, being a wise king, accepted this explanation.

Another legend has it that in spring the nightingale flies around the rose bushes telling of his love until, overcome by their scent, he falls senseless to the ground.

Western poets, clearly influenced by the Persians, have written on the same themes. Byron, for example, called the rose the 'Sultana of the Nightingale'.

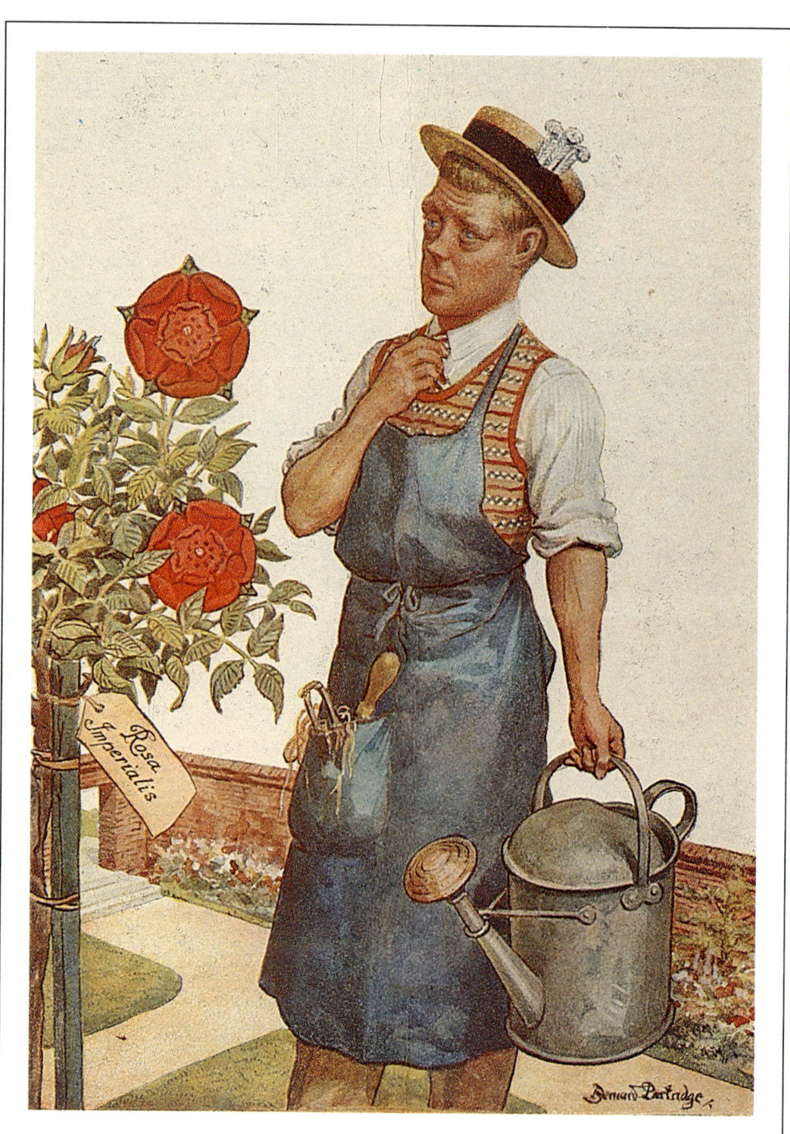
Rosa
Imperialis
Bernard Partridge

The Prince of Wales Watering Rosa Imperialis

Bernard Partridge

English 1861–1945 Private Collection

Bernard Partridge was one of the best-known English cartoonists of his day, much of his work appearing in Punch. Perhaps his most celebrated drawing featured two royal personages, Kaiser Wilhelm of Germany and King Albert of the Belgians. The Kaiser tells the King the latter has lost everything, and the King replies: 'But not my soul.'

The Prince of Wales shown in this drawing later became England's only uncrowned King, Edward VIII. As Prince of Wales his most important activities were the visits he paid to various parts of what was then the British Empire. Partridge's drawing is a tribute to the work the Prince did in the imperial cause.

The British royal family in the present century has included a number of keen gardeners and, in particular, cultivators of roses. Queen Mary, consort of King George V, inherited a love of gardening from her father, the Duke of Teck. One of the chief delights of Regent's Park in London is Queen Mary's rose garden.

After his abdication the Duke of Windsor created an English garden with many roses in France. Prince Charles today continues the royal tradition.

The rose features in the name of the present Queen's younger sister, who was christened Margaret Rose.

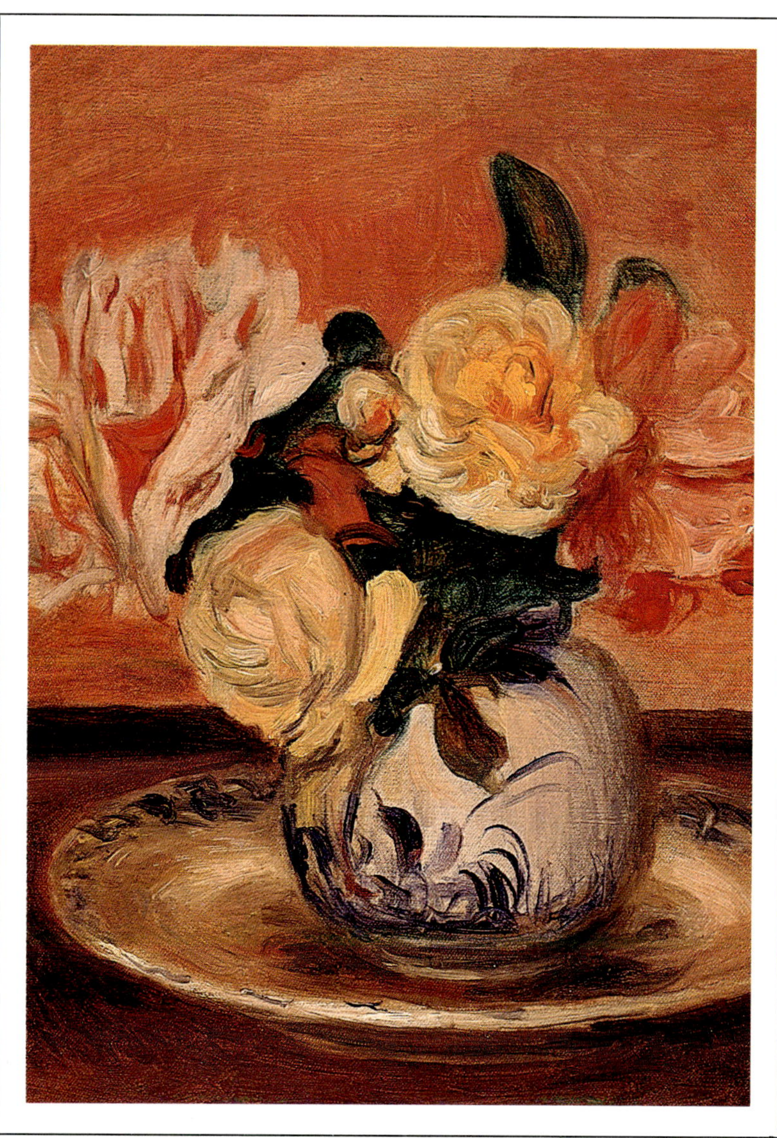

Vase of Flowers

Pierre-Auguste Renoir

French 1841–1919 Private Collection

Renoir delighted in painting both women and flowers and, among his flowers, roses were prominent.

One of the greatest of the French Impressionist painters, he introduced into the Impressionist technique the so-called 'rainbow palette'. This was limited to pure tones at their maximum intensity.

The rose was closely associated in legend with Venus Aphrodite. One explanation of why roses are red was that Venus pricked her feet on the thorns as she looked for her lover Adonis after he had been killed. Another was that her son Cupid, feeling mischievous, emptied a cup of wine over them.

In yet another legend roses were said to have been created from Venus's tears; another has it that they were a gift from the gods to celebrate her rising from the sea.

Pink roses, it was believed, became so because Eve kissed a white rose in the Garden of Eden and it blushed with pleasure.

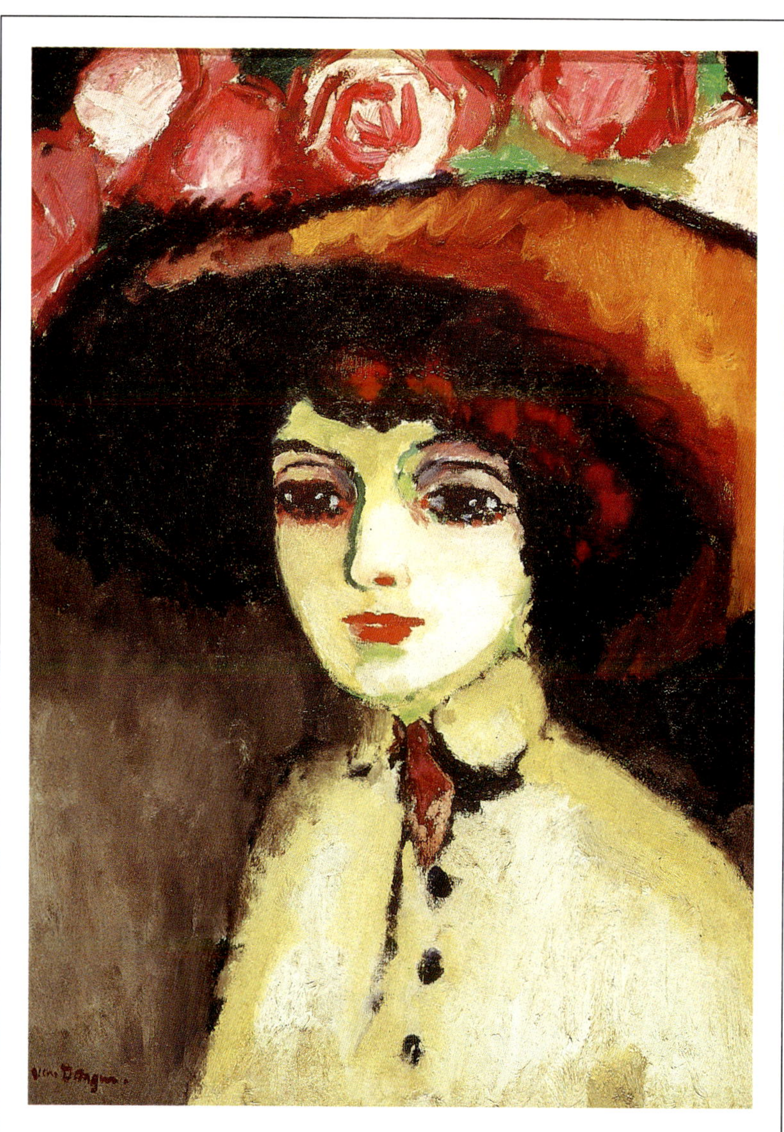

The Parisian of Montmartre

Kees van Dongen

French 1877–1968 Le Havre Museum

Van Dongen was born in the Netherlands, but he spent his working life in Paris and became a French citizen. He made his reputation as a painter of fashionable women, whom he usually portrayed in provocative poses.

As in this painting of the girl from Montmartre, flowers such as roses are used today to adorn women rather than men. Almost the only exception is the male practice of wearing roses or carnations in buttonholes.

In ancient Greece and Rome the tradition was different – garlands of roses were often worn by men at banquets and were awarded to victors in battle.

In times of war in ancient Rome the wearing of rose garlands was the privilege of soldiers. One civilian who defied this rule was a money-lender named Lucius Flavius. During the second Punic War in the second century BC he was unwise enough to look out of a window in broad daylight wearing a chaplet of roses. He was condemned by the Senate to a prison sentence for his offence.

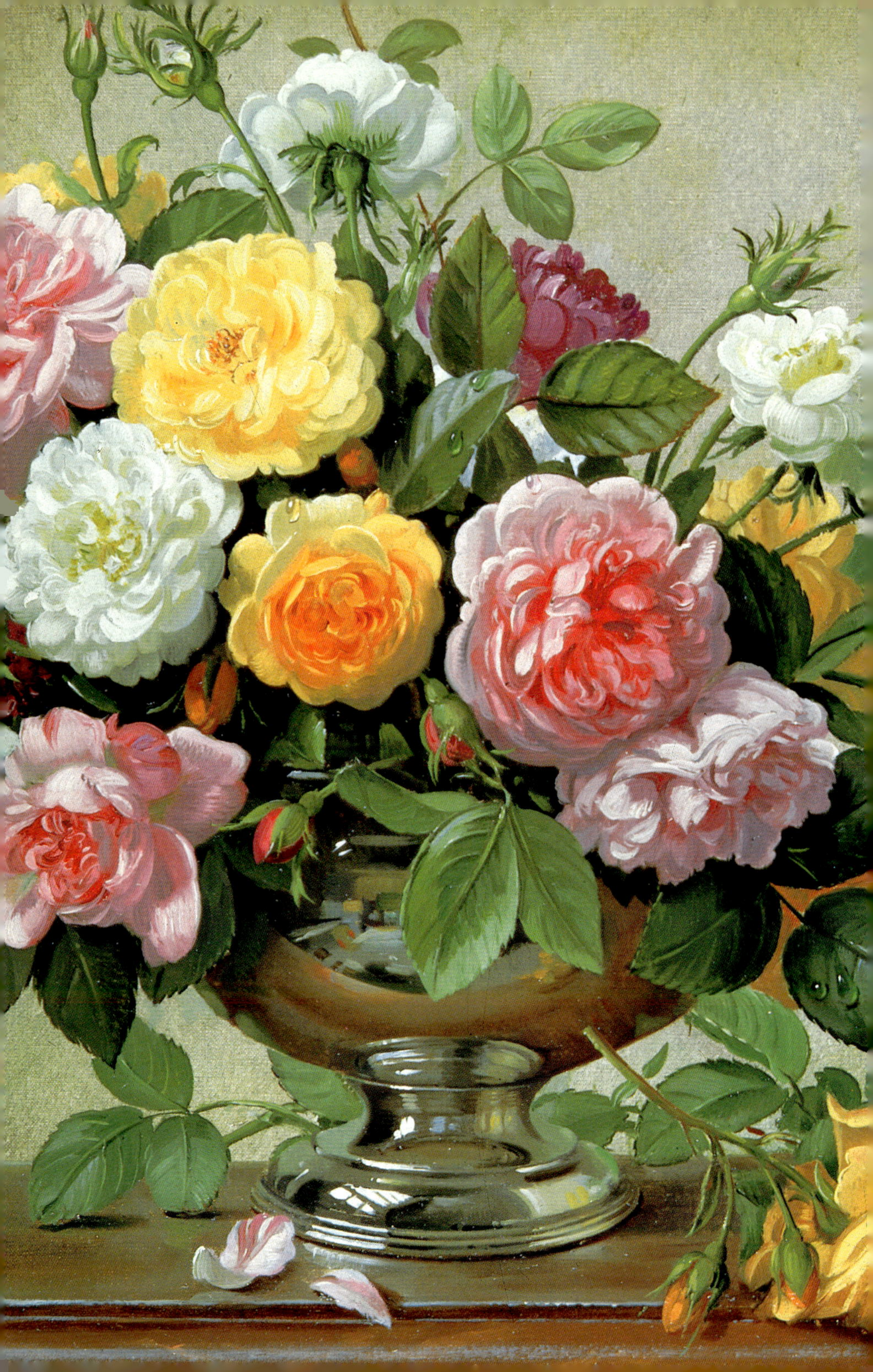

Roses in a Silver Bowl

Albert Williams

English 1923– Private Collection

The rose is so varied in colour and shape, as well as being rich in symbolism and meaning, that, not surprisingly, it has inspired artists through the centuries. Albert Williams's painting is an example from the twentieth century.

One of the qualities that the rose symbolizes is silence. At one time it was common practice to hang a rose from a ceiling in council chambers to indicate that the proceedings were confidential – hence the expression *sub-rosa.*

In dining-rooms, too, roses were painted on ceilings as a warning to guests, and in the sixteenth century it became the custom to place a rose motif over confessional boxes.

By the same token, the emblem of the Society of Rosicrucians, a secret society which originated in the Middle Ages, is a cross covered with roses.

According to legend, Venus presented Cupid with a rose, and Cupid in turn gave it to the god of silence. This was Harpocrates, and the implication was that Cupid gave him the rose as a bribe not to betray either Venus or her lovers.

There is certainly evidence that the rose was accepted as a symbol of secrecy, or silence, or discretion, as early as the fifth century BC.

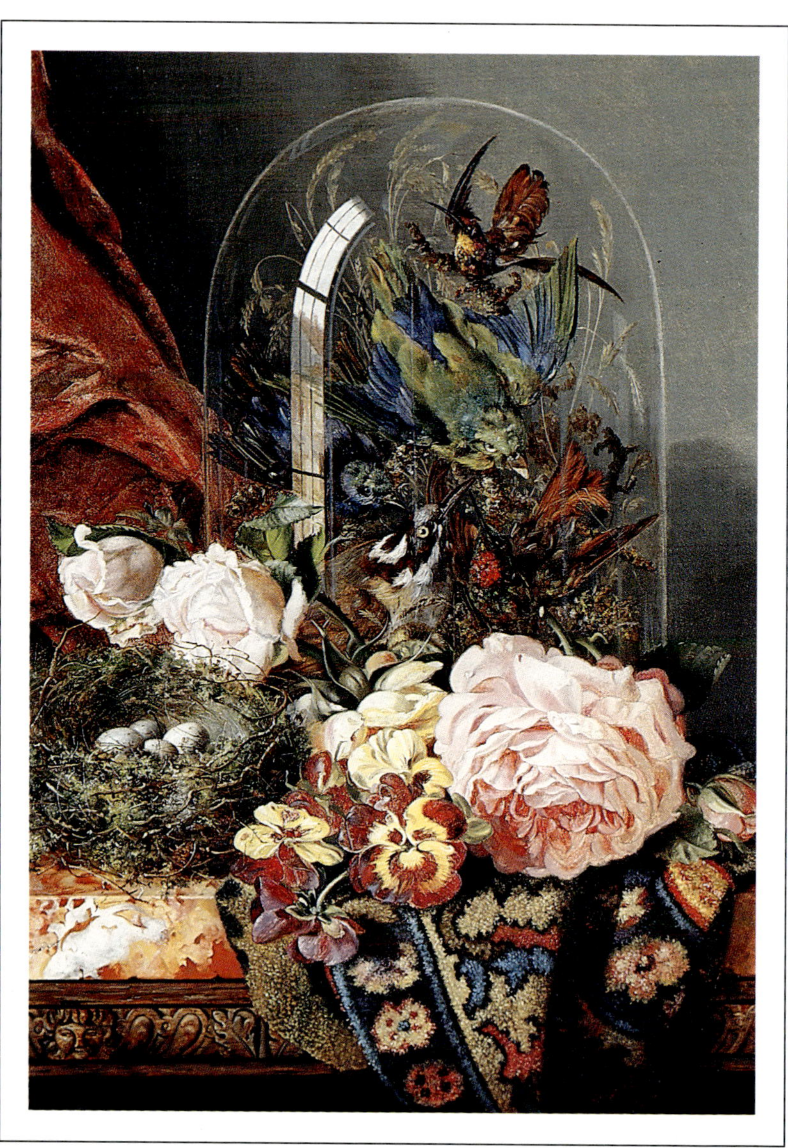

Roses and Still-life

Ellen Ladell

English fl. 1886–1898 City Museum, Bristol

Most of Ellen Ladell's pictures are still-lifes, usually featuring a table with a Persian carpet and flowers on it. The dried flowers and stuffed animals under a glass dome were a common Victorian form of decoration.

Roses, which are seen in many of her paintings, have appealed to the human imagination more than any other flower.

Of the many legends in which roses feature one of the more picturesque was recounted by the Jesuit poet René Rapin. The rose, it was said, was originally a Grecian Queen, whose beauty aroused the jealousy of Artemis, the huntress. Artemis's brother, the sun-god Apollo, scorched the beautiful Queen so that she ceased to be a woman and became a rose.

Sources

HARLEY MS: *The Lover Attains the Rose*
British Library, London

ROYAL MS: *Abelard and Heloise*
British Library, London

The Wilton Diptych
National Gallery, London

LOCHNER: *The Virgin in the Rose-bower*
Wallraf-Richartz Museum, Cologne (Bridgeman)

HILLIARD: *Young Man Among the Roses*
Victoria and Albert Museum, London (Bridgeman)

BRUEGHEL: *Roses with Diamonds*
Galeria dell'Accademia Carrara, Bergamo (Bridgeman)

MURILLO: *The Flower Girl*
Dulwich Gallery, London (Bridgeman)

HOGARTH: *The Graham Children*
National Gallery, London

BOUCHER: *The Marquise de Pompadour*
Wallace Collection, London

FRAGONARD: *Storming the Citadel*
Frick Collection, New York (Bridgeman)

REDOUTE: *Rosa Gallica Regalis*
The Royal Horticultural Society, London (Bridgeman)

LE BRUN: *Marie-Antoinette*
Historical Museum, Versailles (Bridgeman)

HERPFER: *The Wedding Party*
Christie's, London (Bridgeman)

PAYNE: *Choosing the Red and White Roses in the Temple Garden*
Birmingham Museums and Art Gallery

MANET: *Roses and Tulips*
Bührle Foundation, Zurich (Bridgeman)

FANTIN-LATOUR: *Roses*
Private Collection (Bridgeman)

BARO: *Wedding of the Sheikh of Tangiers's Daughter*
Private Collection (Bridgeman)

PARTRIDGE: *The Prince of Wales Watering Rosa Imperialis*
Private Collection (Bridgeman)

RENOIR: *Vase of Flowers*
Private Collection (Bridgeman)

VAN DONGEN: *The Parisian of Montmartre*
Le Havre Museum (Bridgeman)

WILLIAMS: *Roses in a Silver Bowl*
Private Collection (Bridgeman)

LADELL: *Roses and Still-Life*
City of Bristol Museum and Art Gallery